D1523067

Happy Anniversary

WELLERAN POLTARNEES

LAUGHING ELEPHANT   MMVII

LAUGHING ELEPHANT

www.LAUGHINGELEPHANT.COM

Traditional Gifts

1st WEDDING ANNIVERSARY
PAPER

2nd WEDDING ANNIVERSARY
COTTON

3rd WEDDING ANNIVERSARY
LEATHER

4th WEDDING ANNIVERSARY
FRUIT or FLOWERS

5th WEDDING ANNIVERSARY
WOOD

6th WEDDING ANNIVERSARY
CANDY or IRON

7th WEDDING ANNIVERSARY
WOOL or COPPER

8th WEDDING ANNIVERSARY
BRONZE or POTTERY

9th WEDDING ANNIVERSARY
POTTERY and WILLOW

10th WEDDING ANNIVERSARY
TIN or ALUMINUM

12th WEDDING ANNIVERSARY
SILK or LINEN

13th WEDDING ANNIVERSARY
LACE

14th WEDDING ANNIVERSARY
IVORY

15th WEDDING ANNIVERSARY
CRYSTAL

20th WEDDING ANNIVERSARY
CHINA

25th WEDDING ANNIVERSARY
SILVER

30th WEDDING ANNIVERSARY
PEARL

35th WEDDING ANNIVERSARY
CORAL

40th WEDDING ANNIVERSARY
RUBY

45th WEDDING ANNIVERSARY
SAPPHIRE

50th WEDDING ANNIVERSARY
GOLD

55th WEDDING ANNIVERSARY
EMERALD

60th WEDDING ANNIVERSARY
YELLOW DIAMOND

75th WEDDING ANNIVERSARY
DIAMONDS

Congratulations, on this the
anniversary of your marriage.
May the good things in your lives
blossom ever more abundantly,

$\mathscr{A}$nd your home continue
to offer nourishing peace.

May the small actions of daily life be fulfilling rituals.

Let the changing days and seasons
please each of you in their
own way.

May you continually open doors to ever-new adventures and discoveries.

$\mathcal{L}$et there be, in your home, much good talk,

Frequent laughter and joyous play.

$\mathcal{M}$ay your home be a place
where simple pleasures abound,

And peace and silence
have their places.

$\mathcal{L}$et there be, for you,
uncounted moonlit evenings,
and as many sunny mornings.

*B*e like trees, standing together against all weather, growing separately, but next to one another.